Tennis
LEGENDS

Erin Butler and Jared Siemens

MEDIA ENHANCED BOOKS

AV²

BY WEIGL™

ADDED VALUE • AUDIO VISUAL

AV² provides enriched content that supplements and complements this book. Weigl's AV² books strive to create inspired learning and engage young minds in a total learning experience.

Your AV² Media Enhanced books come alive with...

Audio
Listen to sections of the book read aloud.

Key Words
Study vocabulary, and complete a matching word activity.

Video
Watch informative video clips.

Quizzes
Test your knowledge.

Go to www.av2books.com, and enter this book's unique code.

Embedded Weblinks
Gain additional information for research.

Slide Show
View images and captions, and prepare a presentation.

BOOK CODE

W 7 7 3 2 6 7

Try This!
Complete activities and hands-on experiments.

... and much, much more!

AV² by Weigl brings you media enhanced books that support active learning.

Published by AV² by Weigl
350 5th Avenue, 59th Floor
New York, NY 10118
Website: www.av2books.com

Library of Congress Control Number: 2016956747

ISBN 978-1-4896-5266-9 (hardcover)
ISBN 978-1-4896-5267-6 (softcover)
ISBN 978-1-4896-5268-3 (multi-user eBook)

Printed in the United States of America, in Brainerd, Minnesota
1 2 3 4 5 6 7 8 9 20 19 18 17 16

122016
113016

Project Coordinator: Jared Siemens
Designer: Terry Paulhus

Photo Credits
Every reasonable effort has been made to trace ownership and to obtain permission to reprint copyright material. The publisher would be pleased to have any errors or omissions brought to their attention so that they may be corrected in subsequent printings. The publisher acknowledges Alamy and Getty Images as its primary image suppliers for this title.

Tennis LEGENDS

Contents

AV² Book Code 2

History and Culture 4

The Grand Slam 6

Tennis Equipment 8

Greatest Legends 10

On the Court 12

Money Makers.....................................14

Grand Slam Tennis Courts 16

Coaches and Officials.........................18

Grand Slam Winners 20

Quiz..22

Key Words/Index 23

Log on to www.av2books.com..............24

History and Culture

Tennis is a game with centuries of history. The earliest version of the game was played in the twelfth or thirteenth century in France. Back then, the game involved hitting the ball with the palm of the hand. By 1870, the game was called lawn tennis and had official rules. The first Wimbledon tennis tournament was held in 1877 at the All England Croquet and Lawn Tennis Club, as a way to raise money for club repairs. Today, the Association of Tennis Professionals (ATP) organizes the men's professional tennis circuits, and the Women's Tennis Association (WTA) organizes the women's professional tennis circuits. The International Tennis Federation organizes the Grand Slam tournaments. Major tennis championships are played in Great Britain, the United States, France, and Australia.

Ivo Karlović is one of the tallest players in tennis. He is 6 feet 11 inches (210 centimeters) tall. His height allows him to deliver a powerful serve.

In tennis, "doubles matches" allow partners to team up and complement each other's skills. Competitive doubles matches were first introduced at Wimbledon in 1884.

Etiquette

In tennis, **etiquette** is very important. Tennis etiquette is known as "The Code." It describes the behavior of players and **spectators**. The Code encourages players to show respect for their opponents. Every tennis player should show respect for their opponent's time and skill. For example, a server should not take too long between serves, and should only serve when the receiver is ready.

Strawberries and Cream

The favorite treat at Wimbledon's food stands is not the standard hot dog or soft drink of most other sporting events. Instead, tennis fans enjoy strawberries and cream. This tradition is said to go back to the very first Wimbledon tournament. Since then, the dish has become even more popular. On average, Wimbledon fans eat more than 61,729 pounds (28,000 kilograms) of strawberries and 1,849 gallons (7,000 liters) of cream every year.

White Clothing

Tennis players traditionally wear white during matches. This tradition dates back to the time when tennis was a game reserved for the rich. White was a hard color to keep clean, and it implied that a player was wealthy. Today, many clubs and tournaments allow players to wear different colors and styles of clothing. However, some tournaments, like Wimbledon, still require players to wear white.

The Grand Slam

In 2016, Stan Wawrinka of Switzerland beat Novak Djokovic to win the 2016 U.S. Open. It was his third Grand Slam title.

There are four major tournaments in professional tennis known as Grand Slam tournaments. These are Wimbledon, the U.S. Open, the French Open, and the Australian Open. A player who wins any one of these earns a Grand Slam title. Players who win all four titles are considered Career Grand Slam winners.

The U.S. Open is the most **prestigious** and important tennis tournament in North America. It is held every year in Flushing Meadows, New York. It includes women's singles and doubles, men's singles and doubles, and mixed doubles. U.S. Open matches are held on hard courts made from **synthetic** materials.

The silver trophy of the U.S. Open is distinct from the other major trophies because it is larger. Winners are able to take photos with the trophy and travel with it on a media tour around New York. They are not allowed to keep the trophy.

GRAND SLAM RECORDS

16 YEARS — Tracy Austin and Martina Hingis are both the **youngest female tennis players** to win a Grand Slam title in the singles category.

17 TITLES — Roger Federer has won the most Grand Slam **men's singles titles**.

25 TITLES — Margaret Osborne duPont has won the most **U.S. Open women's titles**, winning in singles, doubles, and mixed doubles.

98 MATCHES — Jimmy Connors has won the most U.S. Open men's singles matches.

101 MATCHES — Chris Evert has won the most U.S. Open women's singles matches.

Championship History

The first official U.S. Open was held in 1968. This new competition allowed both amateurs and professionals to compete. An amateur named Arthur Ashe competed in the competition that year. In the final match, Ashe beat another rising amateur star, Tom Okker of the Netherlands, to become the first African American to win the men's singles title. For the rest of his career, he remained an outstanding player. He also stood up for **civil rights**, such as those of Haitian refugees, and raised millions of dollars for the United Nations.

WOMEN'S GRAND SLAM SINGLES TITLE WINNERS

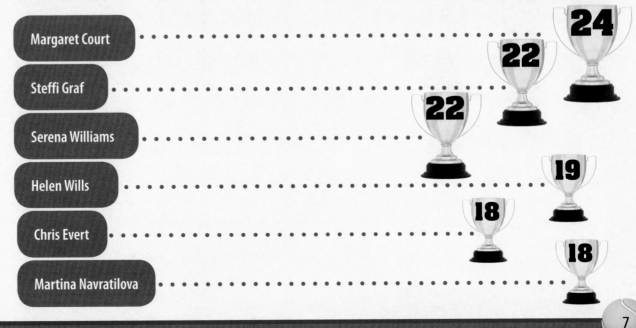

- Margaret Court — 24
- Steffi Graf — 22
- Serena Williams — 22
- Helen Wills — 19
- Chris Evert — 18
- Martina Navratilova — 18

Tennis Equipment

Tennis is not a contact sport, so players do not need protective equipment. Players need only a racket, ball, and a court to play the game. Over the years, these pieces of equipment have improved with better technology. When tennis first began, men wore long pants and shirts, sometimes with a tie. Women wore long dresses with **bustles**. Today, men wear shorts and polo shirts or tee shirts. Women wear short skirts or shorts, and tank tops, tee-shirts, or polo shirts.

COURT

The court is the area where a tennis match is played. Courts can be made out of different kinds of materials, which can affect gameplay. Court surfaces include grass, clay, cement, and synthetic materials. Both singles and doubles courts are 78 feet (23.8 meters) long. Singles courts are 27 feet (8.2 m) wide, and doubles courts are 36 feet (11 m) wide.

Maria Sharapova has one of the best forehand strokes in the game. Her technique has been described as both powerful and graceful.

TENNIS BALL

A tennis ball is made of rubber covered by felt-like cloth. Tennis balls are usually neon yellow or white to make them easy to see. The International Tennis Federation (ITF) states that a ball must have a diameter between 2.5 and 2.8 inches (6.35 and 7.11 cm). It must weigh between 1.975 and 2.095 ounces (55.990 and 59.392 grams).

RACKET

The racket is used to hit the ball over the net. A racket is made of a frame and tightly wound cords that crisscross each other in the frame's center. The ITF requires that a racket be no longer than 29 inches (73.6 cm) and no wider than 12.5 inches (31.8 cm).

SWEAT BANDS

British tennis pro Frederick Perry made the first sweatbands in the 1930s by wrapping gauze around his wrists and his racket grip. Today, sweatbands are made from synthetic, lightweight materials that absorb sweat. This keeps a player's hands and grip from getting slippery. Sweat bands around the head or hats keep sweat out of a player's eyes.

SHOES

The fabric on a tennis shoe is made of lightweight, breathable material. This helps keep a player's feet cool. The soles of tennis shoes are made from rubber or synthetic materials that provide cushion and traction. Most tennis-shoe soles are made in a herringbone pattern, which allows the player to change direction quickly.

Greatest Legends

Even though tennis has been enjoyed for more than a century, it did not become a popular **spectator** sport until the late 1960s. This was due to the major championship tournaments being opened to both professionals and amateurs. This change created what is now known as the **open era** of tennis. Television broadcasts began to feature this expanded cast of players, including champions like Billie Jean King and Arthur Ashe. Famous rivalries, such as the one between Martina Navratilova and Chris Evert, helped draw interest to the sport as well.

Roger Federer

Many people consider Roger Federer the greatest male tennis player of all time. Born in Basel, Switzerland, he began playing tennis at age 8. By age 11, he was one of his country's top **juniors**. He became a professional tennis player in 1998 and won his first Grand Slam title in 2003, at Wimbledon. He has won 17 Grand Slam titles over his career, a record for men's singles. This Swiss player is known for his high levels of skill and grace while playing, which have helped him to avoid injuries. Federer continues to play today and has a large following of fans.

Venus and Serena Williams

Venus and Serena Williams began playing tennis when Serena was 3 and Venus was 4. They were coached by their father on public courts in parks around Compton, California. Venus went pro in 1995, when she was just 15. One year later, Serena followed. Together, they won three Olympic gold medals for women's doubles, the first in 2000, and then again in 2008 and 2012.

Grand Slam Winners

Winning one Grand Slam title is a difficult feat. Winning all four Grand Slam tournaments in the same calendar year is the sign of a true champion. These players have won all four Grand Slam titles in the same calendar year.

Don Budge
1938

Maureen Connolly
1953

Rod Laver
1962 and 1969

Margaret Smith Court
1970

Steffi Graf
1988

Rafael Nadal

Rafael Nadal was born in Manacor, Spain, and began playing tennis when he was three years old. He turned pro at age 15, in 2001, and was ranked number one in the world by 2008. He is known as the "King of Clay" for his success on clay courts. Nadal has won the French Open, which features a clay court, nine times.

Men's Match Wins

Playing consistently in tennis can be tough. Injuries and playing conditions effect a tennis player's consistency. These men have won more tournaments than any other male tennis player.

PLAYER	WINS
Jimmy Connors	1,254
Ivan Lendl	1,071
Roger Federer	1,059

Women's Match Wins

To be a competitive tennis player takes great athleticism. Some of the top female players have won more tournaments than the top men. The women below are the top tournament winners.

PLAYER	WINS
Martina Navratilova	1,442
Chris Evert	1,309
Steffi Graf	902

Martina Navratilova won 59 Grand Slam victories and 9 Wimbledon singles championships. She retired in 2006 at age 49, and has stayed active in the sport as a commentator.

On the Court

Tennis was originally played on grass courts. Today, Wimbledon is the only Grand Slam tournament that uses a grass court.

Tennis has an extensive list of rules governing how it is played. The object of the game is to hit the ball onto the opponent's side of the court in such a way that they cannot return it. The last player to hit the ball within the proper boundaries earns a point. A player must earn four points to win a game and must win by a margin of two points.

The scoring of tennis begins with love (zero points), then 15 (one point), 30 (two points), 40 (three points), and game (four points). Games are played back to back in what is called a set. The first player to win six games wins the set, but they must win by two games. In women's professional tennis, a player must win three of five sets to win a match. In men's professional tennis, a player must win five of seven sets.

Kurumi Nara won her first Grand Slam title at the 2010 French Open, which was also her first professional season. Nara was just 18 years old at the time.

Most Clay Court Titles

Clay courts are more difficult to play on than concrete or grass because they are more slippery. Some players excel at playing on clay. These players have won the most tournaments while playing on clay courts.

PLAYER	TITLES
Guillermo Vilas	49
Rafael Nadal	49
Thomas Muster	40

Most Women's Tennis Association Titles

The WTA was started in 1973. It manages women's professional tennis tournaments, and hosts more than 50 matches each year. These women hold records for the most WTA titles.

PLAYER	TITLES
Martina Navratilova	167
Chris Evert	154
Steffi Graf	107

Most Grand Slam Titles, Men's Doubles

Winning a doubles match takes great teamwork. It also takes **intuition**. These pairs have won the most Grand Slam titles in men's doubles tournaments.

PLAYER	TITLES
Bob Bryan & Mike Bryan	16
Todd Woodbridge & Mark Woodforde	12
John Newcombe & Tony Roche; Peter Fleming & John McEnroe	7 *(tied)*

Fastest Tennis Serves

163.7 MILES PER HOUR **Samuel Groth** (263.4 KILOMETERS PER HOUR)

160 MPH **Albano Olivetti** (257.5 KPH)

156 MPH **Jerzy Janowicz** (251 KPH)

156 MPH **Ivo Karlović** (251 KPH)

155.3 MPH **Milos Raonic** (249.9 KPH)

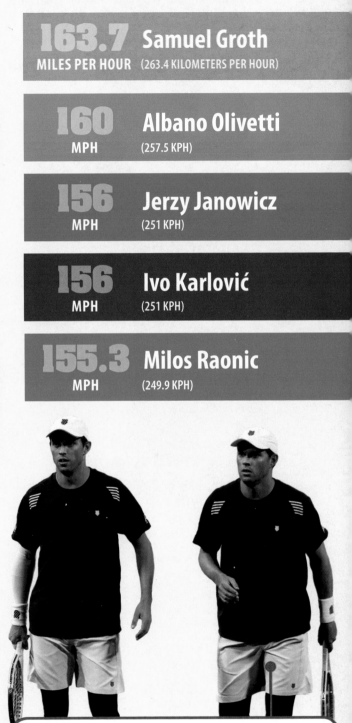

Twin brothers Bob and Mike Bryan were born three minutes apart. They have been playing tennis since they were 2 years old. Together, they have won 112 doubles matches, more than any other men's or women's pair.

Money Makers

Tennis has grown into a multi-million-dollar industry since the open era began in 1968. In total, there is $162 million available for men and $120 million for women each year in prize money. Players earn money both by winning tournaments and by earning sponsorships. Fans support the industry by attending matches and tournaments. Tennis fans spend about $160 when attending a match.

STRAWBERRIES & CREAM
$3.55

VISOR
$30.00

TICKET (U.S. OPEN)
$99.00

T-SHIRT
$28.00

TOTAL
$160.55

Most Career Tournament Earnings

When tennis became more popular, **purse** sizes began to increase. Today, winning one of the Grand Slam tournaments earns a player as much as $3.5 million. These five players have made the most in prize money.

$104.5 MILLION	Novak Djokovic
$98.8 MILLION	Roger Federer
$81.76 MILLION	Serena Williams
$75.5 MILLION	Rafael Nadal
$50.3 MILLION	Andy Murray

Sponsorship

Sponsorship is one of the biggest components of the tennis industry. Companies who become sponsors support both tournaments and individual tennis players. Every year, sponsors contribute more than $739 million to tennis. The biggest sponsor in professional tennis is Aegon, an insurance company, which supports British tennis players and tournaments.

Sporting Salaries

Many professional tennis players today earn millions of dollars. Their earnings come from a combination of sponsorships and tournament prize money. These are currently the highest paid tennis players, including both purse winnings and endorsements.

Roger Federer
$67 million

Novak Djokovic
$55.8 million

Rafael Nadal
$37.5 million

Serena Williams
$28.9 million

Maria Sharapova
$21.9 million

Grand Slam Tennis Courts

Most sports require playing surfaces that are very regulated. Tennis is different. Though the size of the court and the height of the net are the same, the playing surfaces vary. Professional level tennis courts feature clay, grass, or synthetic surfaces. Even the courts where the Grand Slam matches are played vary greatly. This map features four of the best-known stadiums used in professional tennis.

Arctic Ocean

NORTH AMERICA

Pacific Ocean

Atlantic Ocean

ARTHUR ASHE STADIUM
New York City, New York

This stadium is the largest tennis-only stadium in the world, and cost more than $250 million to build. Named after tennis champion Arthur Ashe, it is home to the U.S. Open.

ROLAND GAROS STADIUM
Paris, France

Roland Garos stadium hosts the French Open and can seat 15,000 fans. Its court features a red clay surface and is named after a French national hero who died in World War I.

LEGEND
- Land
- Water

N
W E
S

0   2000 miles

3218 kilometers

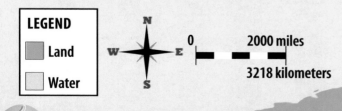

Arctic Ocean

THE CENTRE COURT
London, Great Britain

The Centre Court was built in 1922 and is host to the Wimbledon Championship. It has a retractable glass roof to prevent game delays due to bad weather.

EUROPE

Pacific Ocean

AFRICA

Indian Ocean

AUSTRALIA

ROD LAVER ARENA
Melbourne, Australia

Rod Laver Arena is part of Melbourne Park, which hosts the Australian Open. It was named for singles champion Rod Laver. It was the first Grand Slam arena to have a retractable roof installed for the purpose of shade.

Southern Ocean

ANTARCTICA

17

Coaches and Officials

Tennis coaches make a valuable contribution to the game at every level. Coaches help beginners learn the basic skills and rules of the game. As a player matures, coaches can influence their style and teach them strategy. The best coaches bring players to the top of the ranks.

Nick Bollettieri

Nick Bollettieri is one of the most legendary coaches in tennis. He has worked with an incredible number of top players, including Andre Agassi, Marcelo Rios, Serena Williams, Venus Williams, and Maria Sharapova. Bollettieri has owned and operated a tennis academy since 1978. He is known for his idea of bringing the world's best tennis players together in one place so that they could compete against each other.

Bollettieri Through the Years

1978	Opened the Nick Bollettieri Tennis Academy
1996	Wrote an autobiography, *My Aces, My Faults*
2000	Named one of 50 Most Influential People in Tennis by *Tennis Magazine*
2008	Earned an honorary doctorate for his work in sports
2014	Inducted into the International Tennis Hall of Fame

During his career, Nick Bollettieri coached 10 number-one players.

The Nick Bollettieri Tennis Academy was the world's first full-time tennis boarding school. It is now known as the IMG Academy and has expanded to include eight different sports.

Top Tennis Academies

Tennis coaches often teach in academies. Most tennis academies have built-in schools so young players will not fall behind in their studies. These are the most well-known tennis academies in the world.

ACADEMY	LOCATION
IMG Bollettieri Tennis Academy	Florida, United States
Sanchez-Casal Tennis Academy	Barcelona, Spain
Spartak Tennis Club	Moscow, Russia

Richard Williams

Richard Williams did not grow up playing tennis. After he learned to play as an adult, he started teaching his daughters Serena and Venus when they were just 3 and 4 years old. Serena and Venus have both been ranked number one in women's singles during their careers, and together they have won 15 Grand Slam titles.

Tony Roche

Tony Roche is known as one of the world's best tennis coaches. His volley technique helped Roger Federer achieve his current level of success. Roche has coached several Grand Slam winners, including Ivan Lendl, Lleyton Hewitt, and Patrick Raft.

Brad Gilbert won 20 titles as a professional tennis player before becoming a coach in 1995. He coached Andre Agassi to number one in the world and to an Olympic gold medal.

Grand Slam Winners

Tennis players with Grand Slam victories compete at the highest level in tennis. Many of the sport's best-known players have won multiple Grand Slam titles as well as other championships. Many have also won Olympic medals. For this reason, these athletes are some of the best in the history of the sport.

Serena Williams

22 GRAND SLAM TITLES • COMPTON, CALIFORNIA, UNITED STATES

Serena Williams was just 15 when she turned pro in 1996. From an early age, she was successful in both women's doubles and women's singles. As a singles player, Serena won a Career Grand Slam in 2003. She has won a total of 22 Grand Slam titles, some of them in finals against her sister, Venus. In addition to winning tour championships, she has also won an Olympic gold medal in the women's singles event.

Chris Evert

18 GRAND SLAM TITLES • FORT LAUDERDALE, FLORIDA, UNITED STATES

Chris Evert began learning tennis as a child and became a quick success. While playing professionally during the 1970s and 1980s, she set a number of records, including the most French Open wins for a woman. Over her career, Evert set a record by winning 90 percent of her games.

Martina Navratilova

18 GRAND SLAM TITLES • PRAGUE, CZECH REPUBLIC

Czech tennis star Martina Navratilova was one of the best tennis players in the world in the 1970s and 1980s. Navratilova started playing tennis at age 4. She won the Czech National Championship when she was only 15 years old. When Navratilova won her first Grand Slam in 1978, she attained the ranking of number-one women's singles player in the world, taking the title from Chris Evert.

John McEnroe

17 GRAND SLAM TITLES • WIESBADEN, WEST GERMANY

In 1977, John McEnroe became the youngest man to ever reach Wimbledon's semifinals. He was just 18 years old. He lost in the final round to Jimmy Connors of the United States. In 1979, McEnroe won his first U.S. Open. By 1981, he had won it three times in a row. He went on to win a total of 17 Grand Slam titles, 77 career singles titles, and 77 doubles titles. When he retired in 1992, he had won a total of 856 professional singles matches.

Andre Agassi

8 GRAND SLAM TITLES • LAS VEGAS, NEVADA, UNITED STATES

Andre Agassi was born in 1970 and became a professional tennis player at age 16. Agassi's first Grand Slam title was achieved in 1992 at Wimbledon. He defeated two previous Wimbledon champions, Boris Becker and John McEnroe. The win came after two unsuccessful trips to the finals at the French Open, and one at the U.S. Open. After a long career, he retired in 2006.

Maria Sharapova

5 GRAND SLAM TITLES • NYAGAN, RUSSIA

In 2004, Maria Sharapova was not expected to win Wimbledon. She ended up beating higher-ranked and former Wimbledon champion Lindsey Davenport. She then went on to beat the reigning champion, Serena Williams. The Washington Post called it "the most stunning upset in memory." In addition to her 35 singles titles and 5 Grand Slams, Sharapova has also won a silver Olympic medal in women's singles tennis.

Quiz

Now that you have read about tennis legends, test your knowledge by answering these questions. All of the information can be found in the text. The answers are also provided for reference.

1 In what country did the earliest version of tennis develop?

A: France

2 In what four countries are the major tennis tournaments played?

A: Great Britain, the United States, France, and Australia

3 When was the first U.S. Open played?

A: 1968

4 Who holds the record for most Grand Slam singles titles?

A: Margaret Court

5 What is it called when a tennis player has a score of zero?

A: Love

6 Who is paid the highest salary in tennis?

A: Roger Federer

7 What is the largest tennis stadium in the world?

A: Arthur Ashe Stadium

8 Which two sisters learned tennis from their father and grew up to be champions?

A: Serena and Venus Williams

Key Words

bustles: cushions or frameworks placed in old-fashioned dresses, usually in the back of the skirt, to make them appear fuller

civil rights: the rights of individuals to receive equal treatment

etiquette: polite behavior during a certain event or around a particular group of people

intuition: the ability to understand something immediately

juniors: tennis players who are 18 years old or younger

open era: the time period when amateurs were allowed to play against professionals in Grand Slam tournaments

prestigious: having high status

purse: an amount of money that is offered as a prize

spectators: people who watch a performance of some kind, such as a show or game

synthetic: made from chemicals, not natural

Index

Agassi, Andre 18, 19, 21
Ashe, Arthur 7, 16, 22

Bollettieri, Nick 18, 19
Bryan, Bob and Mike 13

Court, Margaret 7, 22
courts 7, 8, 9, 11, 12, 13, 16, 17, 22

Djokovic, Novak 6, 15

etiquette 5
Evert, Chris 7, 11, 13, 20

Federer, Roger 7, 10, 11, 15, 22

Graf, Steffi 7, 11, 13, 20
Grand Slam tournaments 5, 6, 7, 10, 11, 12, 13, 14, 16, 17, 20, 21, 22
Groth, Samuel 12, 13

Laver, Rod 11, 17, 21

Nadal, Rafael 11, 13, 15, 16
Navratilova, Martina 7, 11, 13, 20

prize money 14, 15

rackets 8, 9

Sharapova, Maria 8, 15, 18, 21
shoes 9
sponsorships 14, 15
strawberries and cream 5, 14

tennis balls 9

Williams, Richard 19
Williams, Serena 7, 10, 15, 18, 19, 20, 22
Wills, Helen 7

Log on to www.av2books.com

AV² by Weigl brings you media enhanced books that support active learning. Go to www.av2books.com, and enter the special code found on page 2 of this book. You will gain access to enriched and enhanced content that supplements and complements this book. Content includes video, audio, weblinks, quizzes, a slide show, and activities.

AV² Online Navigation

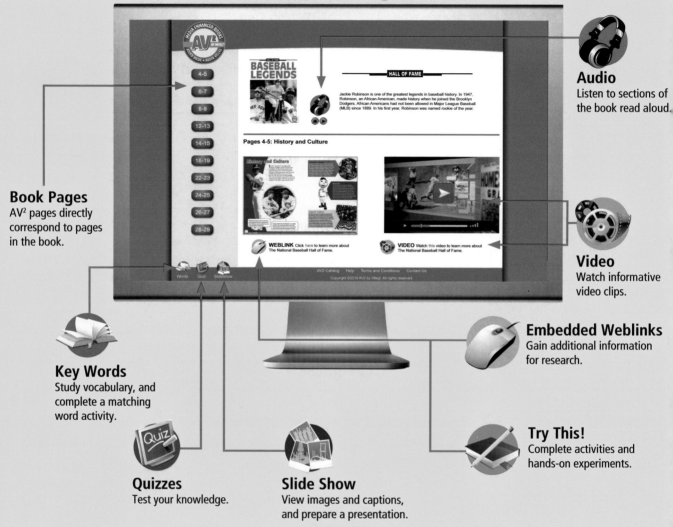

Book Pages
AV² pages directly correspond to pages in the book.

Audio
Listen to sections of the book read aloud.

Video
Watch informative video clips.

Key Words
Study vocabulary, and complete a matching word activity.

Embedded Weblinks
Gain additional information for research.

Quizzes
Test your knowledge.

Slide Show
View images and captions, and prepare a presentation.

Try This!
Complete activities and hands-on experiments.

AV² was built to bridge the gap between print and digital. We encourage you to tell us what you like and what you want to see in the future.

Sign up to be an AV² Ambassador at www.av2books.com/ambassador.

Due to the dynamic nature of the Internet, some of the URLs and activities provided as part of AV² by Weigl may have changed or ceased to exist. AV² by Weigl accepts no responsibility for any such changes. All media enhanced books are regularly monitored to update addresses and sites in a timely manner. Contact AV² by Weigl at 1-866-649-3445 or av2books@weigl.com with any questions, comments, or feedback.